AF408454

SUSTENANCE

50 Poems + One Love Story

SUSTENANCE
50 Poems + One Love Story

Marie Timbreza, MAT

Sustenance: 50 Poems + One Love Story
©2024, Marie Timbreza
ISBN: 979-8-218-45150-9

SKELLOVE WITH GATES
©2024, @eemaart and Marie Timbreza

First Edition, 2024

All rights reserved. No part of this publication may be reproduced, distributed, or transmitted in any form, or by any means, including photocopying, recording, or other electronic or mechanical methods, without the prior written permission of the publisher, except in the case of brief quotations embodied in critical reviews, and certain other noncommercial uses permitted by copyright law.

Printed in the United States of America

Edited by Ilana Krebs
Cover Design by Laura Khayat
Layout Design by Janis M. Albuquerque

"Marie embodies the new-story artist: one that carries her craft into all she does. Whether it be music, poetry, hosting celebrations, or her national healthcare work, Marie's creativity is a bonfire many of us warm our hands by. I celebrate this new book, this light, this collection of flames."
— Barret O'Brien, actor & author

"Marie is an absolutely magical human. As long as I have known her, she's had creativity at the heart of her world— from music to stage to page—her unique lens on the world is undeniable. She loves hard and that love saturates everything she does, centering joy and connection, and bringing out the best in all of us."
— Stacy Bias, artist & activist

"Sustenance is part encyclopedia, part surrealism, part love story, and all gorgeous immersion. Marie tilts the mind, expands it, and shows us what the simple human truths of our lives look like under so many technicolor lenses."
— Cecily Stone, author of These Chasms in the Earth

"Marie, in all honesty, has written more than a few songs on the soundtrack of our lives. She is made of poetry, so everything she does turns poetic. This book is a gift."
— Sue Burns, mother & publisher of We'Moon

❋ ❋ ❋

If the only prayer you ever say
in your entire life is *thank you,*
it will be enough.

— Meister Eckhart

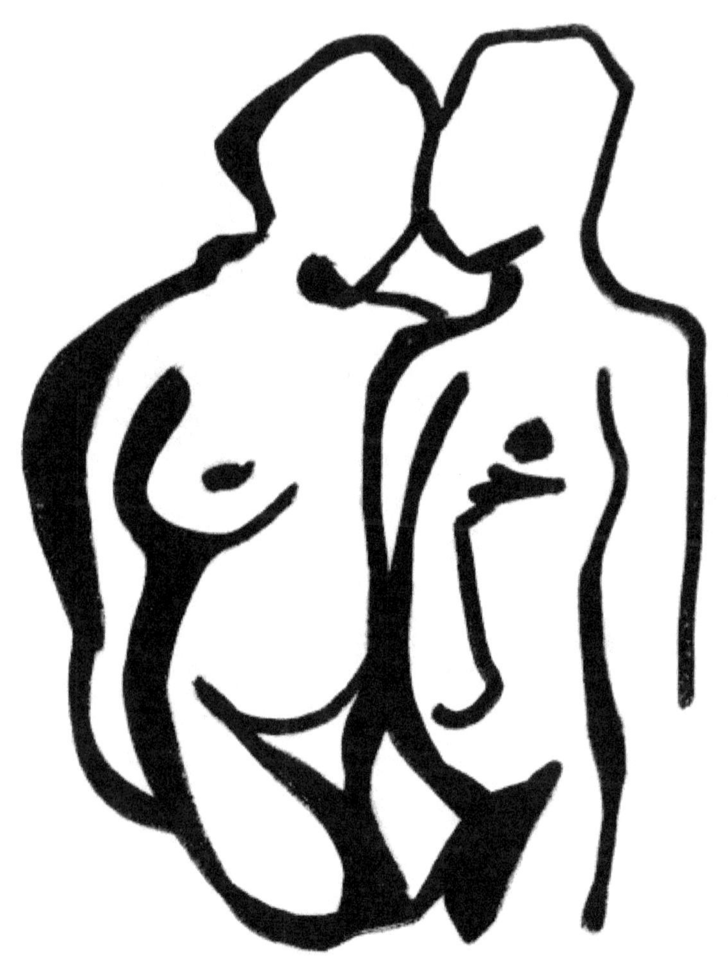

"M&T"
Ink on paper, 2024

Dedication

When I was younger, I wrote of a life that was worthy of the stars, friendships that could rewrite the darkest tales, and battles that could only be fought if great love wins. The stories I learned fueled the stories I wrote, the songs I sang, and the life I have been lucky enough to live.

We found each other and the world became gentler and calmer, a place where we could feel all the feels and hold space for each other with compassion and passion combined. Our love has allowed us to bask in sun, laze in shade, swim in the cool waters, rest under the soft silver of the night sky, laugh with the children, share with the friends, show up for family, and stand side by side in the light of day. I am in grateful service to the love that we share, and I treasure the home that we carry wherever we are.

These doors swing wide as we return from adventures with all the wild tales of what we have learned or collected, what we've lost or let go, and what hopes we hold for what is next for us. These 19 years with you have been the heart of my heart. I wrote of a love like ours, an epic love, a love that sustains.

I love you, T

Marie

Merci beaucoup

- ⚜ my brilliant and inspiring stepdaughters, Emma and Caitlin, I have so much love and respect for you both. It's been a gift to grow together.

- ⚜ my brother Robert, who reminds me to be proud of my story and to *laissez les bon temps rouler*, and my sister Michele, whose immense talent and trajectory helped shape the course of my own.

- ⚜ my parents, Ed and Eileen, who taught the three of us curiosity, resourcefulness, the value of reading, the importance of the right shoes, how to pronounce *Tchoupitoulas* and caramel, and how to make red beans, boiled crawfish, and a roux.

- ⚜ the tender work as a family advocate in organ donation, where our team navigates the complex beauty of grief and trauma to take what is lost and find it a new home. You have also done this for me.

- ⚜ my mentor and touchstone, Jana. Thank you for the kind attention you have given to grow this wild vine into a garden.

- ⚜ Aunt June (RIP), Lola and the Oliviers, Zach, Jackie, Erin, the Nietos, teachers, counselors, and so many others who shared their kindness in the chaos of youth.

✤ The artists, musicians, writers, and rabble rousers who
remind me of *The Why:*

Dale, Fox, Sonora, Kuehnert, Kourtney, Lea, the magic
Wand, Stacy, Mandy, Mary, Ken, Alison, Amy, Julie,
Meg (RIP), Sharon, Mike, Danny (RIP), Genevieve,
Hilary, Susan, Tammy, Andrea, Barret, Rachelle, Jeff
and Hayes, Sean, Karen (RIP), Gina, Doe, Neill, Matt,
Kay, Penny Post/Neutral Ground, Borsodi's, Ruta Maya,
Mojo's, Haven, Electric Lounge, The Fresh Pot, Nikki,
Jos, Emily and Sal, Elisa, Heather, Sue, Rach, Sunny,
Staz, Mitch, Sadie, Beth, Cobalt, Dana, Liv, Shaz, Jami,
Kalen, Marcia, Roz (RIP), Book Woman, In Other Words,
indie and feminist bookstores, bell hooks, Pride Foundation,
Planned Parenthood, TJFP, Sister Spit, The Lesbian
Avengers, Guerilla Girls, TLW (RIP), Rebecca, Patty
and the Gaby n Mo's crew, Megan, Lisa, Kat, Annamarie,
Vero, Tristan, Shannon, Val (RIP), Koonce, Paige, Sam,
Katie, slam teams and bandmates, publishers who
take risks on new works, and all others whose good
work moves us forward.

You are each a powerful force in the world, and we are
all the better for it. Keep it up.

✤ ✤ ✤

"Percolating"
Ink on paper, 2019

Amy Pedersen had a friend who wrote a story about adventures they shared, but in reverse order, including their names. *eema* was born out of that story, and is still trying to get back to the beginning.

She dedicates all that she does to the inspiration that is her wife, Julienne Pedersen.

Find her work @eemaart or randomly on display in the Pacific Northwest.

Table of Contents

How It Ends

Illustrations

Preface

Writing was my first love. I didn't know that it was the love that would set the bar for all others, but it did. It was adventurous, exploratory, exciting, sublime, complex, challenging, humbling, inspiring, grueling, passionate, and devastatingly gorgeous. I would ride my bike to Milton Latter Library on St. Charles Avenue in New Orleans and spend hours reading everything from art books and short story collections to how-to manuals and the *Guinness Book of World Records.*

I knew that there was a world out there that was much bigger than my own, and that I wanted to both take it all in and make a meaningful contribution. I wanted to be a part of something.

The library was a key to many hundreds of doors. In the early 1980s, we didn't carry phones or computers with us everywhere, we wrote things down on paper and folded them by level of importance: the smaller the note, the smaller the pocket, the more important the message.

We left trails of tiny white scraps from tearing sheets from spiral notebooks and taught ourselves how to fold pages into Fortune Tellers, Envelopes with Pull Tabs, Note Squares, Footballs, Triangles, and Bows. If you were lucky, you had the *really good notebooks* with perforated pages so your edges would stay crisp.

Library books were checked out using a paper card inserted into a paper sleeve in the front or back of the book, and things were written instead of typed. It was a time of maximum inefficiency, folding pages back and forth to make a clean tear, and practicing cursive on a different page before you wrote your perfect "LYLAS" or "BFF" on the front flap. Everyone knew the best pens and pencils, the highest quality notebooks for chronicling day to day life, and whose hand-writing was whose. If you passed a note, it crossed the room through several hands, a folded, cursive bucket brigade to put out any fire in any classroom. Note passing was a skill and a badge of honor. If you couldn't get the note across the classroom without getting caught by the teacher, no one trusted you with anything after that. You may as well have told a secret over the intercom. Good luck running for office one day.

Eventually, the notes became stories, the stories became poems, and the poems became love letters, journal entries, bitchfests, and memos to a later self. *You can do this. You have no idea how good you really are. Go for it. We've got you.*

These writings were transcribed from hotel napkins, DIY chapbooks, diaries with soft leather covers and wraparound straps, composition books filled with ink drawings and feminist cartoons, sketch pads with quick portraits and concert tickets memorialized with Scotch tape, and a couple of fine-line Sharpie diagrams of constellations and magical objects to help conjure what comes next.

These poems are pulled from teen years and young adulthood, from times of indecision, hope, gratitude, and asking for help while trying it on my own.

It is a scary thing to put work into the world that cannot be edited once it's printed, but there is also a beauty in honoring that thing you wrote that one time. There will be other books and other stories, but this one cobbles together youth, yearning, and a little bit of how I got this far. This collection of writing honors the imperfect and the impermanent, the art of figuring it out.

Think of this as a few travel notes, some art by the fantastic @eemaart, and a love story of two humans who were lucky enough to land on the spinning marble, in the same place, at the same time. Writing was my first love, but our love is the story, our best work, and my sustenance. ✤

How it begins

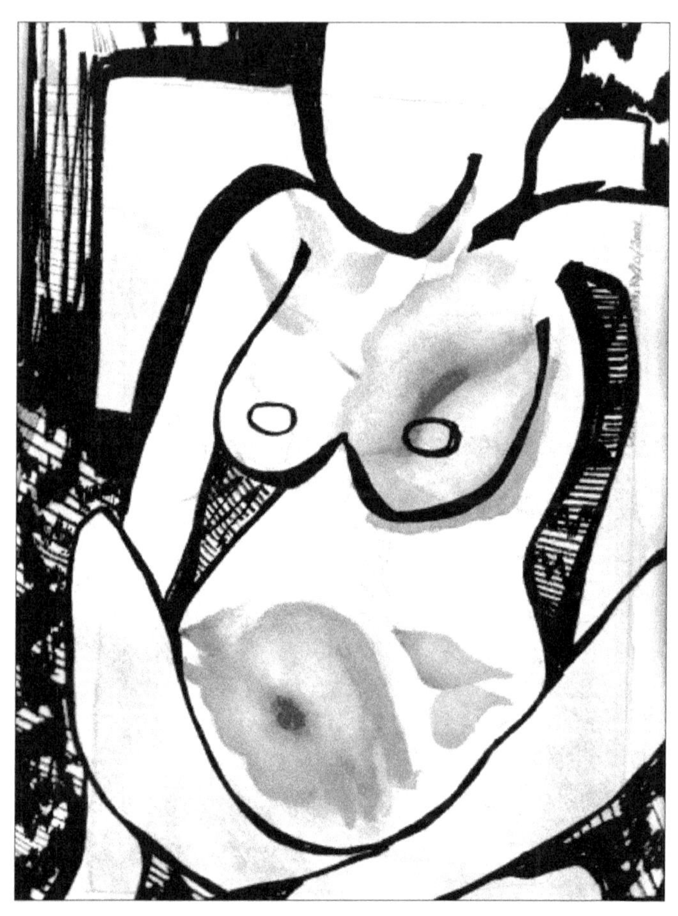

"How It Begins"
Ink on paper, 2019

Sparrows
1997

I wonder if the sparrows
remember as we do,
side glances and fidgets,
first feedings, big storms,
mothers warming, fathers gathering,
nests, baths, wise elders, foolish cousins,
family meals, foolish elders, wise cousins,
feet bruised from bad landings.

I wonder if they know their invasions
are possible ends,
if things they treasure most
are kept close,
nestled beneath
the pale, molted down.

Who was I to you that day?
Was I the one who came or the one who left?
Was I the whipping winds or the flood that
followed?

How does the flying creature
tell the tale of the creature
who walks and runs?
How does one with smooth, tender skin sing
of feathers?

Do they dream of flight?

I ask if the sparrows remember as we do.
You do not hear me, your face
framed in feather and bone,
all the answers safe in your flanks,
your penny eyes shut
and dreaming.

I have moved on to other things,
early morning writing, linguistics as sport,
Sun Magazine, cold brew, stretching.
Things are looking up.
I don't think you could get to me now.
Not here, with my beak tucked
beneath this dark, soft wing.

After Winterson

2000

We want to believe everything. America is at the center of
every map. Every country that ends in an "A" is the enemy.
Enemies are all spelled in CAPS so we don't forget them.
RUSSIA is covered in ice all year round and their children
are taught to drink the blood of American soldiers. CHINA
is dense and green with overgrowth. There they are taught
martial arts and how to live off rice and pepper. Do not speak
to either. They can kill you with a stare like Medusa. They
will cut off your head and put it in one of their Red Squares.

Who comes up with these things?

History will repeat itself, stuttering, *CCCan I ppplease hold
your hhheart in my hhhands? Ppppplease. I lllllove you.* Fear
makes us frozen. Frozen in time. We cling to details like
warmth, like they will be the facts that get the RUSSIANS
to release us, and those CHINESE, well, they won't know
what hit 'em. La Femme Nikita and I will slip through that
slit in the bricks and get the letter safely to the Queen. The
Queen is everything. Everyone in the country loves her.
No one knows her favorite color.

*I was born to love you. Loving you is heaven. I could die in your
arms. I will love you forever. Love is blind. Only the blind can
truly see. Seeing is believing. I could make a believer out of you.
You are my sunshine. Good day sunshine. All good things come
to an end. Anything good is worth waiting for. The good life.
Life's a bitch. Bitch enough and you become one. One in a million.
One size fits all. All or nothing. All together now. Now or never.
Never again. Again I ask you. You and me, baby. Baby. BABY.*

This city is beautiful, gray on a slant with just enough rain
to make you wish for coffee or wine. The library is filled with
men reading newspapers in different languages. The clock is
the biggest I have ever seen, round and sanitized, and hung
where only those not rushed can see it.

You have always been early, but never prepared.

Liza says that the problem is that there are so many princesses
and so few princes. There are a lot of frogs. She says that in
RUSSIA they won't kiss in a doorway. Something awful will
happen. The RUSSIANS will storm in and yell at you with
loud, guttural noises and long, gleaming swords.

We never kissed in a doorway, ever. I swear. No hats on
the bed. No broken mirrors. No walking under ladders. No
drinking from chipped mugs. No doing any of those things
you've heard about from all those other people's ancestry
either, just to be on the safe side.

You don't want any more bad luck than you have already.
Bad luck means you'll lose your keys, your rent money,
your lover, your mind. Bad luck is a brilliant idea and a
pen out of ink in a country where, *"Pen?"* could mean you
would like to marry his daughter and steal his land. Bad
luck is needing a shekel and a half for the only water-closet
this side of Galilee. Bad luck is paying to get in and it's
full of shit already.

The idea of therapy is tracking. *Track the wound back to the
initial injury.* Trace the shape of the very deepest part of the
scar. Follow the blood. Look for scattered bits of silk sheet
and baby dress. Look for the tiniest blue buttons you have

ever seen. This is where it began. Blue buttons from a tiny, baby dress and sheets of blood from the bed where the heart slept.

When you reach a point of taking all that you can take, then it is time to give.

Go back to the house and drink a glass of water, no ice. Go around the corner to the left and find the tree that looks like a woman standing on her hands. In the crease there is a vial. In the vial is a letter.

The letter says that love is coming, but three things must be found first. *I only had two when I found you.*

Go behind the tree and tap your right foot six times. Be certain to not laugh. To laugh while doing magic is to try and pocket fire. Magic hasn't the patience, she will kill you if she pleases. She hasn't turned anyone into a toad in years, she hasn't the time. She will send you away. She will steal your breath and give it to the fireflies. Breath and fire need the same things, and she will like the fireflies better than you, I promise. Leave the tree and walk toward the river.

There is a belltower in the schoolyard. Up the winding stairs there is a black gate with bent hinges and a lock. Don't bother to pick it, it's broken. Kick it open, hold your breath for four seconds, and pull three things from your pockets. Hopefully you brought what you need.

Leave the letter there.

❧ ❧ ❧

After Stein
1996

I — Outing

Well . . . is she a lady or is she One Of Those? I don't know,
miss, I haven't done much talking to her about it, and I don't
think she'd go telling me if she was.
She doesn't *have* to tell you, you can tell by the way she
walks down the street.
How, miss? She don't swang herself there and back, if that's
what you mean.
No. I mean a good, decent man could walk by and she would
be more interested in the cracks in the walk.
Mebbie she's shy, miss. I seen her make special point of
talkin' sometimes.
To men or women?
Oh. Yeah, miss. I see what you mean.

II — Wishing

Coins in a well. Coins n a wel to tel.
To tell?
Yes. A story, yes. In a wel. Stories.
Coins in a awell?
AHEM. yes. Then wishes, voices, n frogs.
two or more. n then more frogs n
pollywogs. And?
Seasons. Seasons down gone. down .
In the well?
YES.
Of course. How silly of me to question.

III — Leaving

A part, apart, depart a
Part. a pice. Peace depart a p iece E. slow. Tap. T ap. T a p.
Mother. Other M. Queen.
Wean, Q;A; my moth rrr
Other jump
Swag kick feed feed
Scream, there.
Their blood. Other An.
Cry, Writ. horse-bit
Juniper. One tramp led
Flower, and you.

❀ ❀ ❀

After Mayakovsky
1996

Prologue.

You sit with me, and I listen to your voice,
crackling among the bark and the leaves,
too loud for this space.

I

They will come for me soon,
for I am not a woman of correct manner,
having never been with child,
thirty-odd and never-wed,
not a woman, but a survey of their fears.

And you! Seeping, sly, one of them. One come from the
pale and sickening television light, escaped from your
den to run the night, paws flattening a path while a chase
persists, until we come to this.

You attack those who cannot fight,
until now. There will be no more wins for you.
The sound was large and horrible.

II

If they wish, I could
let down my hair
and free my chickens
and claim madness,
so that they may each take a piece of me,
take my heart,
my son,
my word for it.
Flapping like a flag in the breeze,
I could stand hilltop and north point,
so that come dark, the star
will halo my head, and they
will drop to their knees and
cry, AVE AVE AVE.

❧❧❧

after cummings
1996

Austin; this hot May   or may not
     listen closely, carefully   the hills

next to which your slender knowing
takes me, She wonders of my rivers

bank   she said   bank and market along
now, long and prosperous to you sir you,
madam, mad am, I
hope that Dusk comes and
You decide to release
     (at least one of)your stars
(for you long I have tender waited)

held these hills have   your special part
your hush tease fur silk. Your frivolity
I know
intimately

❖ ❖ ❖

After Apollinaire
1997

I
        stepped from the edge of New
           Orleans to be
                    closer
                        to you.
Then
        from the bank of
themightychargingmisstowardsissippithehills
        I heard
a
        small
            child
               singing to

               an elder woman
                  smiling   s
                              s
                  at the t   o
                    of
                  wildflowers
                  beckoning water
                    from
                the
                        wind.
I gazed into the wet color.   I saw your eyes.
        I began to notice   my breath.

❧ ❧ ❧

After Oliver
1994

We stroll paths, ducking low
branches, dodging falling leaves.
I am aware of the danger but wish to be
aware of the rest.

The crunch of my soles on the gravel
alerts the forest birds of my arrival.
Oiseaux de la forêt, I want you to know that I
have studied the *Birders Code of Ethics.* I
know that I must promote you, support you,
avoid exposing you to artificial light
or bulb flashes.

It has been impressed upon me that
I should not advertise the presence of a rare
bird, and any mention of rare nesting birds
should be to the proper bird authorities only.

Group birding requires special care and
an agreement on prudent behavior.

Birds of prey, exotic birds, seabirds,
shorebirds, forest birds, game birds,
hummingbirds, marsh birds,
wading birds, and waterfowl
all tilt their heads
with appropriate skepticism.

We should not be trusted, but can be amusing
from a bird's eye view.

We are reminded to look closely
for the raptor's aerie and
listen dutifully for the triumphant cry
of a landing crane.

Amidst a humming city, I sit
in the optimism of delight,
writing my list of
wild things seen and heard.

What words do I have that
could deliver justice to this splendor?
Magnificent
that flight and song
are both born
of a language
that you and I share.

❋ ❋ ❋

Witchcraft
1998

I

I read once that witchcraft should be a secret.
I tell no one of works in progress.

II

They scoff at hexes and potions.
They say that witchcraft is tricks for fools. They deny
the moon her spotlight.
They envy the beauty of other women.
They revel in the taunts of men.
They deny the existence of
spells and incantations
as their bubbling wishes boil over,
reaping more from the night than they ever dreamed.

III

An art book has the face of David on the
cover. Inside, women are yanked and pinned by the
stone that is their flesh and
the men that are their gods.
Rape.
Centuries of the same shit glorified
as the righteous work of man.

IV

She stared at the sketch of the temple
while children hopscotched around her.

They laughed and glanced nervously
at the dark-haired girl drawing.
They moved too fast for her
to shade their eyes.
Later they wore makeup and smoked cloves and
wrote notes to each other's evils.

V

Her hand sped over the page; a woman nude, an
enormous winged *maybe* pressing her lips to
another's thigh, charcoal and wishes created a
woman . . .

A woman reading tarot.
A woman praying to gods that do not rape.
A woman summoning the goddesses that do not
judge a witch.

Sometimes the bothersome
wretch begins to whine and
bitch and whine and then she stops
to think and to sing.

There's a man reading his own work,
a man drawing from his own story,
a man not looking outside of
his own knowns.
Don't follow the guy who isn't leading.

The picture is there, in the air,
until you see it, two bodiless faces pale and talking.
She becomes bitter and smokes and skips and swells
like a small, important dam.

She's heard this before, but can't remember
when or from where.

It could've been just there, right there.
It may have been the retelling
of the death of the martyr,
again.

The wretch is there, there she is,
gawking at the bug-covered streetlight,
staring at the halo of insects,
listening to her own fluorescent gurgle
as her fury dissipates into sadness.

She's heard this song before,
dissected for a beckoning few,
glaring, buzzing, humming.
Fluorescent death does not frighten flies,
just kills them.

These are the poems of a troubled child.
These are the stories of death courting
forever. This is what happens when corpses sing.

This is the story of the whore on the hill.
This is what Persephone left in her will,
just after, *Do not turn back, I shall follow.*

The day looms, like an unfinished sickness,
a wet wall, slowly drying.
She cries and waits, a pitiful wretch
in dear of a return to the womb,
where things are dark and hidden,
covered by primal need and raw want.

The fear, of course, is that someone
will drop us and we will
split like a melon,
as if the Gods were not in our favor,
as if I were not meant to find treasure
nor you an island.

Worry, worry,
mad with its own history,
deluded beyond regret,
much too folded for love.

People ask questions,
not of those who might be right,
but of those who might answer.

You expected nothing and everything.
She delivered.
Just wait until the end.
Big finish.

Aria.

❀ ❀ ❀

Switch Places
1997

This is the part where Persephone
slaps the back of my head and says
loudly, "I'm coming. I'm right behind you."

This is the part where her mother tells her shadow
to remove her shoes and face the wall,
where I hear myself saying,
> *How lovely,*
> *You don't say.*

I wonder if the one person can just
switch lives with another person
when the trigger is pulled or if
the easiest life is easiest only
because they didn't notice the hard,
or if mothers and daughters inevitably
switch places
or call it quits.

Somewhere a girl stands
counting the pearls of her choker
in silent rage,
> *How lovely,*
> *You don't say.*

❖ ❖ ❖

To Be Continued
1997

Don't ask me to answer
hypothetically, I may change under
pressure.
You are an unspoken, enormous whisper
broken over the hull of a ship.
You are glass in the water
and a scent of what is done and coming.

I carry you like a vision of
something I do not have
and cannot see.
A ship crushes miles of water
without apology.

The sea is known
by the how
and the how much,
the tide, brine, and bounty,
the swell and the depth
and the clarity.

Each turn atop waves
is roulette, but because
we are more us than it,
we expect good fortune.

I chanced something here,
a reckoning, a spirit coming in the dark.

Your reaction to the opening
was to touch it,
place it in your pocket,
save it for later.

So here we sit,
you writing to an old lover,
me studying the ruins of Rome.

Funny how we refuse to let this end.

Head

"Vibrant"
Ink on paper, 2024

Bed Full of Books
1998

I sleep with my bed full of books,
like a raft, like the aftermath of a war,
the fight submerged,
the ship now flotsam.

You will meet others,
line to line to page to page,
fumbling, mumbling
in the sheets of my raft,
no jetsam in sight.

I am here with my heroes.
Their tales find easy rest
around their spines,
wrap close around their hero bones.

They know that I listen when they speak,
and that is a powerful thing.

Winterson's *billets-doux* stacked to my right,
cummings flecks of fancy on my pillows,
Silverstein's aunt mabel
staring down the monsters
under this bed full of books,
afloat, like a raft,
like the aftermath of a war.

Eyes close, and suddenly there are chants.
Audre Lorde beckons me to walk through,
Eyes up, she says, Go, Woman she say, GO
Now And Take Peace With You.

Lucille carries the children away
to tell them,
to sing to them, to promise them
the oldest Clifton that she can excavate.

Sometimes she tells them,
sings them, yells them,
promises them as I rock
back and forth and back,
on this raft with so much to say,
pages turning over and over.

Our Lives Are Open Books, I say,
and two women laugh.
Olds and Rich are there,
drawing each other's chalk outlines.

Plath has been tracing Sexton
since the year I was born.
They are at every crime scene,
writing obits.
They always play dead.

Madam Rice unlaces her bustier,
chants, *Off With The Wigs, Off With The Fangs,*
this is a place where Beauty hangs.

No, we can't pull aboard
the desk or the chairs,
no clunky makeup mirror here,
only heroes and you,
plus a carry on or two.

Winterson, hooks, cummings. and Lorde.
Walker, DiFranco, Gibson aboard.
Hold on tight, you know this drill,
unless you slept through it.
You laugh, but you will.

The sheets are creased where lyrics rock me
to sleep, *You Are Beautiful, You Are Enough.*
and, Do Not Fear, All Your Heroes Are Here,
on this bed of everything you have ever read.

Watch your step, honey, look,
it's a raft and door.
Knock, then hold on,
there is room for one more.

❋ ❋ ❋

Sobriety: for the boys back home
2020

snap shuffle kick ahhh
step
into where I live
into where I
step
live and in person
find colors to be true colors
without
ratta tat tat kick slide
step
smearing into hypnotic
charcoal smash into the flames
gray and grayer jump
start by crawling crying scream
begin to walk again laugh again
step three four step maybe I'm alive
step five answers
six begins to swing from the trees
dragging questions calling
through thick history and
miles of highway
STEP

carefully and notice everything
this does not have to be a struggle
STEP
with determination, nothing is taken
for granted
STEP
where the ground is not paved
look where the sky is not the brightest hue
and surely there, on the ridge
will stand a Lakota woman
in a shawl the shade of wheat fields
shouting
STEP
where your God can see you
STEP
where there is no shame
walk where there is no railing
shout where there is no sound
step softly when time calls for quiet
listen
your life calls your name

✾ ✾ ✾

Stories from War: Petro

2000

Of all the men I killed in battle,
only one haunted me.
The hill had cleared of weeping women
and those who feigned death for survival.

I went back to him and wept. *Dominus Flevit.*
I do not recall the year,
but the day is seared into my flesh.
I still smell his blood.
Today is the anniversary.

Six men were there with me,
a pack of rage and despair.
Petro was the only soldier.
He had only one good eye.
He taught us to shoot,
to mark and unmark trails,
to cook with no fire, to drink leaves.
His skills became our leader,
and we watched him,
certain that without him we would die.

All at once, men fell like night. Six on six. I had my
knife drawn to cut cord.
He was around my neck, and I was not breathing.
I swung my right arm back
and hit his temple.
He threw my knife, twisted my head,
hoped to break me.

I reached up to his throat
and squeezed life from him,
like juicing bamboo.

Do not be impressed.
I am not strong, only angry.

The others scuffled, Petro screamed.
Petro crushed his man with a heavy rock.
I imagined him to look like his mother,
or his eldest child.
I wanted to be done with it.
I wanted to collect the camp and leave no trace.
First light split the clouds as I buried him.
Petro left his man belly up on a flat rock.
Petro is angrier than I.

Sky handpicks light for the day
as we name our battles after women,
and slyly hope
for more honor than shame.
We left Isabelle.
From then on we saw her
only in thin nightmares.
Men jump from trees.
Petro screams us into war.
You have affected me this way.

✳ ✳ ✳

Eliza
1995

One morning, Eliza returned from the dreaming
with the residue of *World Beyond*
salting the sweet of her lips.
She could recall, only faintly,
the sounds of singing,
the call of the mourning dove.

On her breath passed the whisper of a fairy tale,
a young girl and a stranger with a story to tell.
He was ancient and mysterious,
with talk of a later time,
something about a metal shop
and a sculpture of the universe
with its clicks and ticks and whirs.

Eliza shifted in slumber, and the story changed.
The stranger became a holy man.
He walked with two others in the desert toward
something soon to be a sun, a star.

Wearing robes and colored sashes
around their waist and heads,
they reached a waking Eliza
and a rumor about the men of the East
gone much too far.

Wildflower
1998

Wildflower, you
move in a way
that reminds them to dance
in the wind,
find sustenance in soil.

Your tender petals call for
special surroundings, befriend the wind
through a haven of hills
and soft-stepping deer.

You are made of spirit
        sunlight
        wind
I look forward to our walk
in the dreaming.

November 19

International Men's Day is November 19. This is
the one day a year where men are celebrated and
spotlighted in society, government, family
structure, pay equity, academic tenure, skilled
labor, corporate, career advancement, and every
level of athletics.

On this important November day, men are put
first, heard clearest, given the microphone, handed
the keys to the kingdom.

We round up on this fall day to ensure that men
have the space to practice their favorite pastimes,
pursue their options for financial stability,
and carefully select their favorite meals from the
bounty before them.

Let's be sure that women stand down and make
room, let men's ideas be front and center, and
not take credit for ideas not their own. Let's
shush all those overbearing non-binary world
leaders for a measly day and make them listen to
the not-yet-heard epiphany of the masculine
wallflowers.

On this day only, they can wield their biceps and triceps and
concepts for how they can be better served in 364 other ways.

On November 19, the world steps aside and lets all men
through, untouched, for a solid 24 hours.

For one day a year, all money will display male
faces, all statues will reflect their achievements in
battle and at sea, and movies will show male
characters as primary, with more lines and
more substance. It will be extraordinary.

With applause and celebratory nods, we will usher them into
the world of women and children and animals and nature.

The people of the world will let boys be boys and men be
men, but only for a day.

That's the Thing
1999

That's the thing, right? What was said.
Maybe we thought no one could
fall in love with us,
that we were not loveable,
that we would be alone forever.

We were told terrible things about ourselves,
which became terrible things we told ourselves,
which became terrible things we told others in
terrible ways, by yelling, lying,
keeping secrets, or silence.

That's the rub, right? The trajectory.
The caress to the distress,
the love to the leaving, and
somehow the race is on.
Coin toss for who will leave first
with the most righteous issue,
the least scar tissue.
Rochambeau for who will light the fire or surface
when the smoke clears.

That's the half of it, right? The other half.

There are the worries and wishes,
the limitations that fence the yard.
But there is also the green grass,
the water at sunset,
the light of day,
a meal of your favorite foods,
a swim in water that soothes,
allowing yourself at the table.

That's the skinny, right? The body of work.

Our bodies, a meticulously crafted
survey of their fears
we now peel away
to the feel and the feeling.
We hold close the Yes amidst the years of
No, tell the skin and the bones and the hands
and the gorgeous mind
that if they can just hold on tight,
power through, hang in there,
keep it together just a little bit longer.

We promise to show up.

❖ ❖ ❖

The Things They Say
2014

That's the thing, right? The things they say.

There are worries and wishes
old limitations that fence the yard,
but standing in your heart,
you know when to show up, and how to bring
your best self to the table.

Say No and No again when it is not right for you.
Say Yes and Yes again when you are ready.

In all of the who and the what
and the where and the when,
we know how to do better.

That's the thing, right? The why.

They told us that our bodies
were not as they should be,
meticulously crafted,
boxed for distribution, and
now we peel away to the feel,
hold close the I Love Myself Anyway.

You don't have all the answers,
but neither do they.

Keep looking.
Clear the clutter.
Learn new things.
Ask.
Spend time with people you treasure.
Tell them.
Spend time with people who treasure you.
Thank them.
Make, bake, share what you know.
Cook, look, take it all in.
Give, give, give.
Give back.

Heart

"Reach"
Ink on paper, 1988

Sailing
2023

When I was younger, I believed
that I could write my way out of any storm,
hoist the mainsail with
one or two deep breaths,
and, pen to paper, turn to feel the wind
as I push in or out of or away from.

I believed that there were many of us,
with quill in one hand and halyard in the
other, steadying ships through manic, mighty
waters.

I learned to swim, studied how to dive,
practiced knots and solid footing,
preparing for the downhaul.

Years came and went, the grades, the hobbies,
the boys, the girls, the laughter,
the risks, the wonder, the tears.

I had not yet learned that the leading sail edge
should face the wind.

We took turns at the helm in storms too mighty,
but the dark sky always opened and closed.

The rains always stopped.
My my, what a view.

Every shoreline, each sunset,
all the smiles and songs and laughs,
my home on the water.

A frayed halyard is not good for a sail.

When the sail becomes difficult to raise,
check for jammed or dirty sail strings.
No loose shackles, no loose halyards,
no jammed slugs.

It's all compounded by winch power.
Wear your life vest. Drink water.
Wear sunscreen. Tell him you love him.

Look at the chart before you head out,
check the direction and don't miss the sunset.
That is the why.
The him and the wind and the sunset.
That's how you get home.

Maison
1999

I called her Maison. I don't know what they called
her. When I thought of the years stretched across
my life like a soft, leather-bound book, I thought
of the ranch that I could build with my heart, girl
money, and Maison's hands.

The ranch would be on land, a few dozen acres
with a river nearby. There would be a fire pit and
a huge stage for calling the gods out to play. You
should see how the girls play with Bacchus when
he visits. They get along *just fine.* These are made
of the same spit and fire. The goddesses get too
caught up in making sure everyone is burning sage
or stirring the pot clockwise. The boys just get dirty
and sing.

When I first met her, she said her name, loud and
clear, but a bus drove by and I missed it. It didn't
seem right to ask her again, so I waited until a name
came to me instead. I found it for her quickly, as if
she had dropped it a few blocks back and I returned
it to her, as if I had chased her down.

There is no hope in making up a story about her, so
I simply watch the part of her that makes me sit and
listen. She will sing you into waking. The real glory
is where the story does the making.

I met her in Texas, where grass rolls across the thick,
flat heat without pause. Texas sweats in rebellion
against wind. Texas dares you to breathe while August
is speaking. Just shut up and listen.

I have never known love. All right, that is a lie. I have
held the words of friends like roses to the vine. I carried
them in my arms and felt a familiar weight. I have loved
them as I love the earth, listening to their cries like rain.
I have never known the love that is not seen, but felt,
without hexes or potions or wishing so hard that the
wish gets smashed. I have never known weightlessness,
but I have heard wonderful things. I imagine that it
happens to other people, probably people with money,
or land, or grandchildren. I thought I was weightless
once, but I was wrong. I was fragile, and I didn't know
until I hit the ground.

There is a biological preserve in the Santa Cruz Mountains
that is home to 1,190 acres of protected land that you can't
visit without a docent. There are bats, Argentine ants, and
controlled fires. Originally the ancestral land of the
Muwekma Ohlone Tribe, Jasper Ridge has been a resting
place for many creatures and many stories. We do our best
to make sense of things with the objects we hold and the
tales we know.

When Helen was taken from Menelaeus, I am almost
certain that she was carried by a raptor to Jasper Ridge
en route from Troy. There is no distance too far between
epic tales. Here Helen left a long scrap of red sash and
two black feathers.

I found these feathers when I was 13 and had no idea what
Helen had been through. *How was I to know I was happily
collecting the trail to her rescue?* I thought the feathers were
beautiful and the sash was my favorite color.

Helen stayed with the raptor and wound up loving him.
I gave the sash to Maison but kept the feathers. I was
working on my wings. Perhaps, even then, I knew that
the truest of love was the giving of self, not the giving
of things.

This is not timeless, so I am forced to call upon the Greeks
to give it substance. This is not about faith, so I am called
upon to date it back, back before rocks were rolled or stories
were formed. I must show you a photo, brown, and frayed,
to have you trust it.

I love her. That doesn't seem to get my point across very
well. I LOVE HER. There. Now you can hear it in whatever
loud voice you use to hear important messages. I love her
in all caps. I LOVE HER IN ALL CAPS.

Maison was fixing the wall of a house across the street.
She had strong arms and looked my friend in the eye.
There were reasons that I could count why I would
fight at her side, instantly and without explanation.

There is no search for bravery. It is placed upon you,
like madness, like suddenly falling and dashing your
head on the rocks. Get up. Get up and get ready. Maison
made me braver by standing near me. She would get
me out of heaven if I were to ever be trapped there.
She would get me out.

Love is not easy, but it does make you try new things.
When I next saw her, she was driving. There was a
bridge above, and a stoplight, and me in my car with
her, smiling, feeling excited and calm. I don't know
what other people called her. I felt like I had just run
in after school and someone was waiting to hear the
most interesting thing I had learned that day.

She was Maison. She was home to me.

Boy Hero
1994

My first night home in a year was
the best ever with you.
Every few months, I am reminded
of all that is unbroken,
as hands stroke
and lips kiss.

I have known your eyes.
I become cooler, smoother,
more delicate with you.
I catch, you catch, we toss aside.

It all slides through, and
navigates the passageways,
from the blue of your stare
to the green of mine.

It reminds me of
when we were younger,
sexier, ten times as fragile,
laughing while tying knots
and making promises.

We knew that first anythings
are precious and heavy,
especially this one that is only ours,
ours and no one else's.

Smelling like bike rides
and laughter
and all that is forbidden,
full of defiance and rebellion,
we made fiery plans.

We would ride to your mother's house,
lay in the attic, lock the door.
Key Master, Boy Hero,
fun, sexy story to tell, and
most well-known secret.

We pocketed *The Wild Us*
for stories told 'round firelight,
and rallied every lover since
to be as raucous and brave.

Memory favors you and the
one-by-one afternoons in your attic room
where we fixed broken gadgets,
wrote music,
hid from our fathers,
and often went three rounds
about one thing or another.

Each time I arrived,
you looked at me
like I had finally come
after hours of waiting.

The curve of the river met
the curve of our bodies
and time stood still
while hands kept moving.

In those days,
love's eyes were blue.

❧ ❧ ❧

Rules of the Heart
2001

There is no recipe for devotion.
Its ingredients cannot be bought.

Devotion selects you like bravery does,
and suddenly the cliff is not so steep,
and the last words that confused you
make perfect sense somehow.

You have dashed your head
on the rocks,
and contrary to the blood,
you are all the better for it.

The vessels are a–scream all at once,
the peripheral vision now lassoed
into a dimly lit cavern
where red footprints are left seeping.
The pulse is deafening.

You have entered your own pulpy heart.

There will be a fine for littering.
Please do not write on the walls.
Eat organic so your crap
doesn't stick around forever.

Careful.

Watch for footprints, handprints,
stretch marks.
This is how the heart remembers.
It has a memory of its own.
The rules change with each season.
There are parameters.

No sleeping through the alarms.
No calling past 11 PM.
No calling before 9 AM.
No greeting cards or mailing lists
about congressmen or Catholics.
No guessing how many lovers.
No bossing.
No cilantro or goat cheese or tickling.

I am good to go.

Some things are given.
Some things are taken away,
like breath and third chances
and the last bite of the lasagna
when you have an older sister.

Careful.

You love me, this red footprint, this mess
of pets, lovers, journals, parents,
what I eat, where I sleep, and you.

You of lightning and stream,
you who decide to tell me something
one night in November.

The heart knows that you want us to hold each other,
hold the new us tighter than we hold
the reasons why we shouldn't.

You come into my life
like light filtered through a curtain.
You feel like possibility and passion
and word stew, eaten on a rocket ship,
en route to Mars.

Yes, I wanted to kiss you too.

Buyer beware, we could begin something that
remains undefined and scary to our friends, our
future lovers, to us.
We could defy gravity.

Watch out, I could send you
a plane ticket at any time.
You could have the best time of your life,
get home, and realize that you already know
what you thought you would learn.

You could ask the knock-knock-knock in your
chest what it can teach you.

Listen to the short and long beeps.
Read it back.

You say that you are on your way
to a world without guilt or shame.
I am hoping to do the same.
There are no rules to follow.
There is no recipe here.
The heart is a pot that is constantly spilling over.
The ingredients cannot be bought or sold or
explained in an artistic retrospective:

*Bravery's work was predominantly religious through the early
1000s until politics made a splash on the scene with edicts and
tariffs and hints of blood red in the gray. The first of the Bravery
family to pay the high international tolls was eldest sibling,
Courage, at $1700 per word for unedited speeches to two or
more people in spontaneous assembly. Younger brother, Daring,
gave shame a run for its money in the early 2000s and changed
the face of the game.*

Once things feel out of control, we shift from charting the
course to mapping the origin.
It was all fine until that heart stepped in.

The heart sits in the chest.
The chest belongs to you.

From this point on, Bravery remained entirely separate from politics and found haven in the vast reaches of the open sea. Bravery was also found in some areas of metro Netherlands, with the tribes of Alaska, among random Asian outposts and in remote African medical clinics, and squatted in kitchens in Mexican villages along the Rio Grande. Bravery plans a resurgence in streets outside of American factories and clinics, and in numerous break rooms at companies where money is made but not earned. Bravery speaks truth to power, but who listens, well, that is a toss-up.

Don't rely on rules or promises,
they break too easily.

That heart in the chest
in that body
of that one person you know best,
that is the one to ask.

That is the answer you need.

❖ ❖ ❖

Hands

"Group Project"
Ink on paper, 2023

Hope and Soil
2024

I hoped to be
intentional
innovative
inventive
lucky in my meetings
optimistic in my greetings
selective in my seatings
efficient in my fleetings

I was trying
to be boldly quick
like lightning or wit

I wrote poetry that
flowed from the pen
greedily, hungrily, until
it all started to subside

How do these friendships come and go from us?
How could they ever stay?

I now rely on hunger and hope
in equal measure
love and luck in equal parts
we plant flowers
no longer plucking for a vase

we watch them stock and sway
in their own glorious gardens
we check their soil and their color
and bring shears or shade

I have been taking care of for so long
I have forgotten how to take care

Once the gray winter passes
I hope to have readied my roots
for more soil
I love you like rain
I love you like sun

Morning
1995

A day in the parade
cautious smiles
nervous laughter
bitter cold in four directions

marchers straightening hats
crowds adjusting costumes,
tugging straps as if readying
small, burdened donkeys
with soft brown gazes,
wandering until evening

We should get away this weekend.
We could go to a cabin.

More logs on the fire and presto
            Your arms
            Your jeans
            You are warm
I could dig you
I could take walks with you

Morning,
your crinkled face waking,
this is a kiss

❋ ❋ ❋

At the Top of The Senator Bar with Beth Ann
Toronto, Ontario, Canada
1999

"I'm tired," she said, and her hands held her head
red locks around three silver rings.
"Waiting on people's a bitch," she said.
"Sixteen years and I'm still getting used to these shoes."
Her pumps scraped my boots as she uncrossed her long,
tan legs.

"What do you do," she said, "write?" Her
right hand gestured to my spiral bind.
"What do you write?," she said.
"Poetry," I said, simplifying
my entirety into three syllables,
one word, an easy breath, a tear.
"Poetry," I said again, and laughed.
A slight wind.

She was still, and stared at me,
her body so motionless,
even her jewelry was quiet,
for the time being
what it was.

Beth Ann watched my years
slide down my cheeks.
She did not move. She waited.
She witnessed a cis, white girl
in a cis, white world
be suddenly not so any of that,
fingers stained red around the nails
from twenty years of cheap polish and cotton balls
and late night phone calls,
digging for a heart in the wreckage
of one familiar crash.

Beth Ann touched my hand and winked a glossy eye and
said, "I'm gonna tell you somethin' gonna make you smile,
or maybe just get you to play your hand. I used to be a
man," said Beth Ann, "I used to be a man."

Twenty-five years of being a woman-loving,
word-wielding, fire-stealing, middle-class schoolgirl
didn't seem so bad.

"Cry, child, go ahead. But tell me why."

I couldn't answer her. I had too many questions.
Back to my head I went, where she could explain
the pills and the procedures and the therapy and
the hormones and the riddance of man things,
all man things.

She could cover the purse and the pumps
and the want, so huge and pressing against
her once-upon-a-time man thigh.
"It's not as complicated as people think.
It's pretty simple if you let it be."

I asked her so many questions, I felt I should pay her,
rip the sky where she sat and make mere mention
of rain, to wash clean what my voice had dirtied.
I needed her to explain.

Beth Ann took my hand.

We traded stories of fathers and mothers and
bullies and dark corners where we scrawled
our poetry in bathroom stalls.

She sent me sailing on her first fishing trip with her
boy cousins who laughed at her slight wrists and
precious hands.

She put me in her mother's vanity chair where
we did her hair and nails and disguised her dark,
sweet, boy stare with Maybelline and a cold cream mask.

She said she knew at twenty-one. She knew.
Done as a boy. Through.
She said she started the change.

Silence. Silence.

Cigarette smoke and pumps and glossy stares and silence.

Then a smile.

The schoolgirl says to Beth Ann, "Thank you."
Ten years fall into a humbled lap.
She is the only woman in the room.

"Why do you cry, child?," she says.

"I have been trying to get to my truth for years," I say,
"I have been cutting away everything to get to what I can love."

Beth Ann laughs. Glossy eye.
Wink. Smile.

"So have I."

✳ ✳ ✳

Hands
1994

As I recall, a man
did this once or twice,
not so long ago.

The traffic would shout
to interrupt the well-practiced play.
My eyes would dart to his,
hoping that we hadn't lost it in the noise,
hoping that we could hold it
long enough to taste it.
That's what we're doing here, right?
Tasting and seeing and feeling it, right?

Is this right?
Am I doing it right?

My hands would grip tightly.
Sweat would drip to my collarbone
to dry there, wait to be wiped away
by small, delicate fingers.

I followed the rules
in the monster playland,
looked for my father in their eyes
and turned away, appropriately.
I felt the slow butterfly into my mother,
and turned away, appropriately.

Morning did not filter through the curtain
in such a lovely pattern,
nor did the comforter seem
so deliciously warm,
nor did I hear myself breathing
in time with splendor.

I remember doing this with a man,
but I found something else
in the smooth coolness of your arms,
in the berry red
of your hush tease
beckoning.

❧ ❧ ❧

From April to May
1994

You argued that nature would take its course.
It did, and now you're angry. Why?
Because your world is unpredictable,
and not as in dreams.

Do you remember sitting beneath the peach tree
and retelling the myths by which
we have shaped our lives?
The excuses,
the reasons,
all the little untruths
that we pack each day
for the adventure?

We have compromised everything
for a slot on the board,
a blur in the impressionist garden.

You have collected so many diamonds
that never made it to a ring.
Sometimes the diamond
is the thing.

We have forgotten how to remember.

How it works

"Big Time Wrestling"
Ink on paper, 2024

Stories from Europe: Mata Hari and the Men
2000

The Mata Hari left her husband when she still had three
names like the English. She left him for love, the love of
The Oriental Dance. The Mata Hari would cover herself in
veils and drop them one by one until she danced nude
before them. Men told her everything. Some days she didn't
ask. Some days she didn't listen. She danced. Men adored
her, spoiled her, feared her. The Mata Hari knew everything.
She was every force of nature. She was each element, every
drop of rain. She was sex.

She was tried and convicted of espionage. She was executed
by firing squad. She refused the blindfold. Blindfolds are
worn for the killers. If your eyes are covered, your spirit has
to stay put until they make a clean getaway. If your eyes are
not covered, your spirit jumps from your eyes into their suit-
pockets to haunt their dinner table for the next 600 years. Do
not think you are invisible. I know nothing of love, but spirits
haunting suit-pockets are my specialty.

Life does not begin with breath. It begins with acknowledge-
ment. You are born. Way to get out there. What a champ.
Good job. What a winner. Congratulations. Don't breathe yet.
They'll hear you. I'll tell you when the scary part's over.
Close your eyes. Hold your breath. Hold it or they'll hear
you. If they find you, you'll have to learn to speak and to
cook and you'll never get a moment to yourself. The dead
still breathe. It's just that no one notices. No one pays attention
to them anymore. Death is hearsay. Life is atta boys and
chucks on the shoulder, back slaps and head nods. Alright,
breathe now. Good job. You really are beautiful. You take my
breath away.

If you're lucky, no one will recognize you. But then it happens. Someone offers you a treacherous walk down the longest, darkest alley you have ever seen. You pause. You have heard about alleys. But you go because you are bored. And you think you are invisible. And there's a story waiting at the end of that alley. You can feel it. So you go.

You smash your right hand and blacken your left eye. You lose two teeth and sixty-four dollars. But you run hard and fast, and you come out of that alley and someone sees you. You stammer through the story quickly and they call for the medics. They tell you to sit down. You'll be fine. You did a great job. You are out of breath. Your heart is racing and suddenly you are winning. Do not be ashamed to be hungry. We are not ashamed of the same things. It is not that I want to be fed. It is that I do not want to be misrepresented.

Do not tell them you tried to feed me. You tell them how our eyes looked that night, how our skin moved beneath the moon like water, how you love me easily, like breathing. You tell them the things you said to me, or you tell them nothing. Do not tell them that I am too hungry, or that you did all you could. *How dare you.*

You tell them the whole story, or you tell them nothing.
In the meantime, our love will be in my pocket. You are
too dangerous to have it. With all that dancing and all,
you could say anything.

No one knows which way the spirit goes when you drop the
last veil. Do not sell us as cheap love that will not withstand
winter. The Mata Hari still knows everything she was told.
Our love is not scared of you. We have lived on scraps for
400 years. We have survived Texas summers. She was power.
She was sex. Our skin is tougher than your bite. Things are
whole before they are broken. This hill is steep. I do not need
a blindfold. Our hearts have rolled before.

Fire away.

✢ ✢ ✢

Stories from Europe: The Eye of the Day

2023

Margaretha Geertruida Zelle was born in Leeuwarden, Friesland, in the Netherlands, on August 7, 1876. She was the Dutch daughter of a prosperous hatter who lost the family's money when she was a teenager. After her parents divorced and her mom died, she lived with relatives, attended teacher's college, and married an abusive Captain (MacLeod) in the Dutch army.

After giving her a daughter and a son, her husband gave her syphilis, and amidst the chaos of their treatments, their son died. Some believe the nanny poisoned him, but others believe the mercury from STD treatments worked its way into the son's bloodstream. The couple divorced and she maintained custody of her daughter, but her husband then refused to provide financial support, so she eventually lost custody to him for financial reasons.

Hoping to earn enough money to reunite with her daughter, she danced in Paris under the name "Lady MacLeod." She later took the name "Mata Hari," a Malay expression for the sun, the "eye of the day."

Around this time, she started collecting information from French government officials in exchange for money from German government officials. German secret service officer Elsbeth Schragmüller trained her as a secret agent. Margaretha would make different arrangements, as needed, to pay the bills. She admitted to sharing secrets but claimed that they were outdated and unable to be used.

The French were more upset by her duplicity than her spy work. She was convicted in July, 1917, and died by firing squad in October, 1917. She spent four months awaiting death in a French prison, 11 years married to an abusive husband, and 41 years as a woman who could not dance her way out of debt, deception, disease, or death.

Her story has been told thousands of times, in every country, in many languages. It is the story of women doing the dirty work of men, keeping terrible secrets, losing before gaining, and getting paid to entertain and inform, but not getting paid nearly enough. The price is always too high.

She was a mother who wanted to be with her daughter. Everything else is everything else.

Stories from Europe: Sorrento, Italy
2000

We arrived Friday, May 27, after 20 hours of traveling and waiting combined. Flights included New Orleans to Chicago and Chicago to London Heathrow. *Note to self: Avoid London Heathrow at all costs. What a mess of an airport.* All escalators and queueing pass through tiny doorways, single file, only to get on another escalator and hope it works before the broken air conditioning in the building starts to really get to you.

London to Naples, then Naples to Sorrento by bus, up and down winding cobblestone streets lined with laundry airing on upper balconies, ancient women with tan, carved faces, and the smallest vehicles you have ever seen all buzzing past one another.

We spent 30 minutes on the first evening following haphazardly placed signage for La Lanterna, the restaurant that seemed to have the best reputation in the neighborhood, *"Si, Si, La Lanterna, thissa way . . . thatta way. You will like it. Very good."*

Once we found it, down a tight alley behind the main square,we ordered food, and after a few inquiries about its origins in Sorrento, found out that we were at La Lanterna II, an imitation of its famed predecessor and not nearly as conveniently located as the one that we somehow walked by three times in our sleep-deprived stupor, despite its prominence on one of the four main streets.

The head waiter at La Lanterna II, in silver hair and bright pink tie, alternated between hustling passersby to any open table and taking orders while belting out crooner vocals to no one in particular. When the traveling four-piece band neared the dining crowd, he made requests of them to play songs for him to accompany. It's not to say that his voice wouldn't impress some people, I mean, his enthusiasm alone could have easily won him over with a crowd of Ethel Mermans and Minnie Pearls. That particular night, I preferred a more subtle wooing, a softer ballad that was better for digestion.

We returned to the Carlton International after dinner for some much-needed rest and relaxation. Breakfast in the hotel dining room and then a walk around the open markets of Sorrento's Tasso Square. A hat, a book, post-cards, a beverage and lunch at a pub named after a statue of a cherub peeing. The waitress, Joanne, was English, down to earth, and not a singer in need of an audience. A post-dinner visit to the concierge to arrange the week's trips and get a couple of more pillows. We are a multi-pillow family, it turns out.

Sorrento is a hillside paradise, with tourism at its center, but not at its heart. At its heart are citrus trees and soft leather, stones beneath your feet, and everything that is possible in a place accessible only by winding roads, ferries and hydrofoils.

Sorrento, a known sanctuary for the Sirens, offers you a limoncello, lacework, and marquetry. It also offers you a trip away from yourself, the best trip of all.

❖ ❖ ❖

Stories from Europe: If I Spoke French
2000

If I spoke French, I could tell all these people about you, about how we met and how I was always a little tickled by the way you move, about how beautiful your hands are, and about how loving you filled me from the first day.

I never learned French. I was busy smoking cigarettes and selling things to future frat boys. I feared you and me, scared that we would never be friends, scared that we were friends already.

This is what we have always done, created fear and absolutes. Always. Never. Everything else is sketchy. I have always loved you. I will never love you. I have never loved you. I will always love you.

Everything else is secondary. Right now it is just me on this overnight high-speed train to Paris, scrawling hurriedly under a bulb the size of a camp light while four other women sleep. *How can they sleep with me missing you this way?*

I would have to speak French to tell them. The ripping your heart out of your chest trick is old hat by now. It's all in the cards. If I spoke French, I could tell them how you have always loved me and how you have never loved me, and since the clouds cross the sky without reason, I will stay on this train.

That will show them. I will love you anywhere and everywhere that I am, and they will never forget it.

They will feel that they know you before you arrive. They
will stack the thickest towels and I will slice the fruit myself.
I will be singing when you arrive, and you will hug me, and
your head will find my shoulder. We will ferry about and
drink wine. We will laugh and figure things out as the days
disappear.

The train stops and you are nowhere in sight. I call out to
you and there are too many trees. You are gone. If I cannot
hear you, the world must burn.

Each time I miss you, I want to set something on fire.

Stories from Europe: Esther Sunday
2000

"Here I would like to recount a little story so beautiful I fear it may well be true." — Foucault

Some sort of resurrection, that's what we are celebrating. The day of Esther, the first Sunday after the first full moon after the Vernal Equinox. The Gregorian calendar gave the day to a man and now Esther's Sunday is ripe in the Western world. All the little lambs are bleating and kicking excitedly. Pastel eggs are being hidden and found. Rabbits are being gifted to little, snatching hands across the land.

The resurrection fern is a drought-resistant, evergreen fern found in the southeastern U.S. and tropical America. It appears to be a ball of coiled, dead leaves in the dry season, but revives with moisture. The resurrection plant, however, is a perennial desert herb that curls its stems inward when dry.

It is not the weight of love that frightens me but the weightlessness. We come and go from each other so quickly, like sulfur surrendering to flame. Need launches from one's chest to another's shoulder and perches, awaits all things ambiguous to nibble, store and feed to screeching young.

We learn these ruptured demands from our elders. Their terse longings and convoluted misgivings become our Big Book and all that I know of you becomes all that they know of you, and I am not who I am anymore. I signed on for love, the grandest of all gifts. I have a basket now, filled with candy and toys. All I want is you.

A resurrection gate is the roofed entry to a cemetery where a coffin is paused in transit to its resting place while awaiting the arrival of the clergyman.

It will not be this way forever. It will change with the next tide. We search those narratives of beginning and middle for an end that can cozily nestle before bedtime. Someone will rewrite the story with distant perspective and numerous lessons learned. Things are whole before they are broken. Things read one way were written another. The books we know are not the stories we understand. This was not mentioned in the manual, this art that I must make, this pyre that I must build to burn myself away with each resurrection.

It is not that I am afraid to do this. I have done this before, this molting to move forward. It is that I have never done it alone. I am learning how to do this by paring down to nothing, bringing nothing with me, not even myself.

A resurrectionist is someone who brings something to life or into view again. It is also someone who exhumes and steals dead bodies, especially for dissection. A resurrectionist is a body snatcher.

Esther's body was found buried beneath a mountain of shredded green plasti-grass, her enormous brown hands cradling the sky. Her breath still pushes the ocean, her body curves along the lush, green ridge. I can begin this anywhere along her body, I can fall and die and resurrect anywhere that there is Esther.

I can start here.

❋ ❋ ❋

Pinky Swear
1996

Remember me, Mother?
I was the one who carried you when you were small,
or was it the other way around and around we go,
somewhere across the miles of cornerstones
and around the sharp corners of milestones.

Remember me, Mother?
I am the one that came before to warn you.
I am the one who came after you to tell your story.
I am the one who collects the stories of being alive.
I am the one who is least rocked by death.
I miss you.

I am the one, Mother, the other one, the last one, the listless,
the poet one, the one who could never live anywhere with
more neon than trees,
the one who is strangely certain about abstracts,
like truth, and love, and justice.

Remember?

I am the one who grew from your garden, the one who
noticed the scars on your hands and on your body, the
one who asked their origin story.

I am the younger one, Mother, the one who watched the
rest grow old, the one who remembers the story of your
belly, the *hysterectomy scar.*

I looked up *hysterectomy* to see if it meant death,
or that someone would go blind or deaf or
melancholy.

I found that it meant that there would be no more
children.

I remember that scar best of all because it was the
widest and longest and deepest, cutting all the way
to the womb, where I pictured a sign that read:
Not Zoned for Children, no longer zoned for children.

Perhaps the instant I traced that scar with my tiny
fingers, I knew I would never be able to return home.
I was never to return to a place of dark, swampy illusion,
never again to say, *"I promise mother, I will return to you."*

From that time, leaving home no longer meant missing,
hoping, wishing to return, but stretching, crying,
laughing, breathing deeply,
moving on.

Fields

2000

*"In the widest sense, they signify spaciousness or limitless
potentialities. Into this category come the Uranian gods such
as Mithras, called the 'Lord of the Plains'. He had the task of
assisting souls upon their return to heaven."*
— Cirlot's *Dictionary of Symbols*

The active ministry of Jesus Christ lasted from age thirty
to age thirty-three. Simon said he loved Jesus. Loved him
enough to follow him across the desert for three years, not
that Simon was really leaving anything for good, I mean,
he probably didn't have a girl or a job that he couldn't
come back to if he wanted. Religions always have a back
door.

Maybe it was easier back then to leave someplace for
someplace else. Maybe it was easier when folks would
maybe put you up or feed you or loan you a camel.
Things are different that way. Evangelism is a plague.
I dare you to ask to borrow a camel. Go ahead and walk
across a desert now.

Find anything you believe in strongly enough to do that,
and someone may follow you across burning sand. Maybe
her. Maybe me. Maybe not.

Faith looks different now. Religions are tracts and shares. Someone said that McDonald's is the second largest land-owner in the world, and the first is the Vatican. It's said that the English own Burger King, the Japanese own 7-11, and somehow this skips the news and we rally the troops as they buy charcoal and beer to celebrate America's independence.

Nothing is printed about how I loved you well, how you made me brave, how I held you above me and mapped the sky with your form. You made me shy with wonder. Our conversations are now plotted on the back of your hand. Like an apple orchard, or a math sequence, or religion, you were always more organized than I.

Organized religion means that someone wrote down a plan for a building with a lot of seats. Some up front, some in back, some on pews, some on carpets, some in big, carved chairs. Some get to speak, some do not. Some wear uniforms, some carry the books, the candles, the incense, the law. The leaders tour like rock stars. Famous people wait in lines to hear them speak. Richard Gere saw the Dalai Lama speak and hasn't left his side since. *That must be really annoying for the Dalai Lama.*

Millions waited for John Paul to open his little window at
St. Peter's and wave them into their own personal Jubilee
year. Old women in wheelchairs sat in the hot Roman sun
for hours to glimpse a white robe and skullcap from across
the square. Some had hotel suites with velvet drapes and
a hell of a view. Some were absolved via satellite. My father
and I were in the middle row on Easter Sunday in 2000.
We had already walked through all the Holy Doors of the
Major Basilicas. We were a shoo-in. *You were nowhere in mind.
I didn't think of you in Europe. There are too many other statues.*

They say the best stories are universal. The greatest story
ever told covers everyone. Creation. Betrayal. Family. Death.
Prostitution. Best friends. True love. People used to believe
in doorstep messiahs. Now people have trouble believing
in anything at all. Even love that burns so hot and so bright
it rules our doubt of it. Find something that graces your life
and trust it enough to close your eyes and shut your mouth.
Find a book, a tree branch, a God of your wildest need.

Go ahead, I dare you.

I dare you to believe in me.

✠ ✠ ✠

The Woods
1996

The path in the woods leads to a cabin
where I put my childhood long ago.
I grabbed her hand, *"Run, run now."*
She ran alongside, *"Where are we going?*
Why are we running?"
I could only run, clenching tiny fingers,
hoping the cabin surfaced before the rain
That's all I remember
I haven't seen her since.

I stare into my life and whisper,
"Have you seen her? Do you know where she is?"
I run through trees,
sometimes laughing
sometimes crying
sometimes singing
"It's safe now,
it's safe now,
come home."

❖ ❖ ❖

Red Inside
1997

we have begun to imagine the each
as something other
you   a tattooed ball of fire
with wisdom gnawing at your memory
like rats to rope
me   a hollow mother of
                spoon-smooth hands
                old as gingerbread
and sweeter than our   love

we will forget this
as boredom
clamors in your ribcage
metal crashing louder
than the heart
you have suffered
I know this
you have whispered
I have listened

you fight rage as if
it does not know
your methods or your madness

you forget that she gave birth to you at dawn
and you gave birth to her   with a split and a scream
when the first shrill cry   broke the window
and left   only hands
thousands of them   hitting
slapping   grabbing   taking
more than you had to offer

you will forget what you are here to do
and I will remind you   as our red insides
swirl in the taunt of ecstasy
I found you   and you me.
and we,
        we will forget this

***

Mother's Day at Thirsty Cafe

Cascade Locks, Oregon
2020

My beautiful mama was the human equivalent of *The Giving Tree.* It took years for me to realize that this giving was rarely restored or replenished. My mom gave three children to the planet, 27 years to a marriage, and 34 years to a nursing career. She gave 28,029 days over 76 years to the tedious and beautiful workings of the world.

She gave sarcasm and sparkling laughter and hearty meals and cups of coffee and backhanded compliments and words of encouragement and mentorship, and even an occasional suggestion to head on home so that she could get some rest. In each scenario, she gave until she could not.

When it came time for her to leave nursing leadership for a return to bedside nursing to reduce her stress level, she searched for someone to help her write the letter. My young brother helped her get the formatting just right. I remember sitting on the other side of the big wooden desk, chin in my hands, watching what I would realize much later was the two of them navigating one of the most important letters my mom would ever write, and one of her most poignant moments of self-care.

The amount of doing that mom carried never stopped until it stopped all at once. I spent years wishing for better things for her. In my few years on earth, I had never seen a life so tragically underwater as my sweet mama's.

Her mom passed away when she was three years old,
and her father was a kind widower who owned and
managed a grocery store while parenting four children.
Her older brother died in a car accident while heading
home from the military base on break. My mom said
hat after her mom died, her father spent all of his time
in the store earning money to raise his family, but after
Jack died, my grandfather would take all of the milk
out of the fridge to make room for beer.

My mother held loss in her chest like a second heart,
beating alongside her pulsing life.

Three sisters navigated the world after that, a world
of disappointing husbands and wild, unruly children.
The sisters had each other in the long days, with
steadfast hearts, however broken. They helped raise
each other's children, helped each other find and
keep work, lived either together or near each other.
They gathered in times of joy, grief, celebration,
or emergency.

What To Do Next was a conversation best had over
coffee and dessert, whether or not there was a meal.

There was no time in the history of sisterhood that no action was taken. There have been right actions and wrong actions and really wrong actions, but always action.

Then there was the action needed after the action was taken, the post-action action, which usually involved escalating the solution to the next level: the cousins. The bigger the issue, the bigger the family suddenly became.

It became clear to me at a very young age why the Mafia flourished.

***

Teaching Myself How to Play Piano
and Speak Spanish
2024

I know just enough to get myself into trouble
if anyone needs more than The Pink Panther theme
or the location of *el baño*

just enough to trip on the edge of *el* or *la* or
los or *las* or *ayuda me* or, *y'all go ahead and go,*
I'll catch up

I am now balancing rudimentary scales with
conjugations and chords, but only the minor ones

the major ones are not ready for me
to open the gate and take them on
there is so much to learn
but immersion
at this age
at this age

looks like climbing inside
of the upright, listening
saying *gracias*
and *de nada*
until the song is done

❋ ❋ ❋

How it ends

"Anthem"
Ink on paper, 1991

Do Not Edit My Life
1998

Loving is easier here,
the air between us so ready
to be taken in, given out.
I am beckoned
by her wonder.
I am taken by her giving.

We ask and reply.
We carry on with the intensity
of soldiers who return home,
expectant and ready to rest
in a whole new way.

I never want to forget this moment,
her eyes filled with wins and losses,
the fiery present
of a future protecting her past.

Do not edit my life
for your comfort or your shame.

You tell them that I was
a true lover of women.

You tell them that I took risks,
lived through the evils that men do,
and stood up singing.

You tell them that
I watched over children
with the ferocity of a wolf pack,
that no one was allowed to scar me
once my eyes were open.

You tell them that you loved me
or that you didn't,
but don't you dare pretend
to have known me
without acknowledging
the darkness and light.

Do not forget
to mention the woman
who wears the widow's shroud.

Do not edit my life,
for I will come for you,
with a wild band of women
who have been spoken for.

In your remaining days, you will hear
only our voices, in harmony,
as we endlessly scribble and sing.

Some will nod at my ending,
a pyre and a prayer,
a pen and a sword.

A priest will spite my service,
his neck testing the grip of his virtue
as he prays for his Magdalene.

My face, still full of words,
will feel the cool breeze of the sea,
the heat of each woman who passes,
whispers her struggle
and her promise
to my shadow.

Stories from Europe: Herring
2000

Herring season just ended. They eat herring raw in
Holland. In France, they eat Basque herring with oil
and onions. Atlantic salmon is more rare than Pacific
salmon. Five Pacific for each Atlantic, and the Red
King Crab, well, they sell for 80 bucks apiece.

First class on a high-speed train to Amsterdam,
France, Belgium, Holland, seven boys and me,
scrawling stories in my window seat.

A fisherman is telling the rich boys about his Dutch
find, a bicycle, 150 guilders, Green. He says he left
it in Utrecht. He's on his way to pick it up. The boys
laugh. They say he should have bought a stolen one.
Cheaper, they say. Laugh. Laugh. "It's part of the
Dutch education to steal one yourself, " they say.
Laugh. Laugh. He's not Dutch. He is something
else. He is simple. And he is not laughing.

I am hoping that he talks to me instead, and the
boys will joke and no one will hear them and the
simple man will tell me about his other finds. I wait.

He begins to talk again. He asks them if they have ever
seen a hagfish. Laugh. Laugh. They don't know what it
is. "The hagfish is like an eel, but purple, with a big mouth,
and they are really hard to catch. They burrow inside of
other fish to survive. They are real bastards," he says.
"Those and slime eels," he adds. Slime eels. The boys
were quiet. He's got this.

In Alaska, there are fleets of ships carrying thousands
of men who are not afraid of freezing. These men each
hunt something different and what you make each season
depends on what you catch. On some of these boats, there
are black pots. Pots are 1000 pound traps used to catch the
red king crab. The way it works is that five men lower it
together, slowly, to the bottom. But sometimes it slips.

He says the men are tired from being out there in the cold.
He says the things are fucking heavy, and sometimes, in
the Bering Sea, especially, the men get caught in the traps
on their way down. The best crab trappers have made up
to $80,000 in five weeks. The fisherman says they expect
to lose about 5% of the men each year to the pots.

In Alaska, there's a place called Bristol Bay, America's Fish Basket. During salmon season, the bay fills with aluminum boats. They are 32 feet long, with four men in each, and when the tide is in the men are allowed to cast their nets. They are only allowed to cast their nets when the tide is in, and as soon as it goes out, they stop.

They gather the nets and they wait. For hours they wait. The tide comes in again and the nets go out. The men scramble to catch as many salmon as will fit in the boats with them. It has been said that the boats crash together from the panic. Men have lost fingers to the sharp edges. They say some men lose a finger a season if they aren't careful. They say these are the reddest salmon in any waters. The best salmon. The Japanese love them. They pay well for the biggest ones. They gobble them up. Red salmon eat fingers. The red king crab can eat a man alive.

Merfolk are known to be lonely, vengeful and bored. One cannot play catch too long. Do not be fooled by riches. The sea will not give, only barter.

I, Skyscraper
1996

On the second floor, two people are loving,
moans and groans promising everything, anything.
From here, I see another woman in red heels and
ripped teal silk, screaming about the day she's had.

The check-in list is full, the floors are clean, and the
walls are housing old men's schemes and young lads
dreams of a dripping wet prom night.

Pay for play in seventeen rooms tonight, as I,
Skyscraper, watch them hail, taxis, dropping
off and picking up.

I see those who place heaven high above their heads
climb to the roof of me, scream about how scraping
the sky has other meanings, other meanings that they
insist someone tell them, tell them quickly before they
try to fly. I see all this as I, Skyscraper, watch the bird
men fall.

Like *Scheherazade*, I have tales, 23 magnificent stories,
each next one stacked upon the last for long nights of
entertaining a Sinbad king, my city.

With 2000 glass eyes, I see the sordid lives of men,
watch them glimpse from their suites and comment
on a world at which I stare, all the time, beckoning
the noise and the quiet.

A lady shudders in the north lobby, she senses the crash
of a Boeing jet and does not not understand how or why.

On floor 15, a man sees his reflection and heaves a sigh,
begins to cry.

Elevator holds a family of five, a package of three going
down, plus an elder holding his son's son, both with the
gaze of a boy who was once in love.

A day of celebrating is held in my lobby, a chandelier
is cleaned, and a buffet lunch is steamed for all the
mentioned conventioneers.

Clam chowder is served in shell shaped bowls,
raw fish is the delicacy from Hong Kong,
tasted politely by pursed lips, through which
passed many deals and steals and undetected
lies that day.

I, Skyscraper, in my humble structure and suitable
frame, am responsible for their lives.

I, Skyscraper, am responsible for their lives.

Through the tinted panes of the 20th floor,
an island is sold off the coast of Haiti.

From the east dining room, a toast is made to that
island's diplomatic king.

From the framework to the folded sheets, these walls
have been nailed, painted, sanded, collapsed, rebuilt,
and even shot once when a Muslim congregation met
with a lone fundamentalist teen.

On the fifth floor, a four-year-old boy forgets the room
number he learned in case he became lost in the big
skyscraper.

He cries, but I can say nothing, for I was built to be silent,
and observe.

❖ ❖ ❖

If God Came to You
1998

If God came to you, sat atop your television, one lip bloodied, one eye bruised, and spoke, in her ancient whisper, "What happens now?"

You stare, your mind scouring the kitchen tiles, your hand groping the couch for the remote control needed to end the conversation.

What if you could look upon her, see creation in her woman-flesh, as your angst-filled fist rips the bluish glare?

What if you felt your own hand slowly beckoning
the precious gentle of her sigh? Are you afraid?
Do you know that nothing holds less than nothing?

Look at what you have

done.

She crumples on the carpet, testing you, waiting
to free the horses when your limbs are tied to
their stamping feet.

What if God were a woman?
How much hell would you have to pay?

A Dedication While You Are Still Alive
1998

I would like to write a dedication
while you are alive, and read it to you
while you are barely listening,
so that I can work on my hesitation and inflection
and pause when you look up and notice that
I am still here.

I can shift my weight from foot to foot
and stroll from observation to proclamation,
and then read it to you again when you are
listening closely.

I would like to write a poem in honor of your voice,
the first time I heard you laugh,
saw you cook, cry, fold laundry,
give time to someone who needed it most.

The hope is to really scribe your vibe,
to catalog an epilogue, to honor and jest about
what makes you the best.

But I can't stop to jot down
what I am living alongside you,
because what I might miss
would be tragic,
and the magic is
everywhere that you are.

✳ ✳ ✳

The Gates
2024

The Tibetans may be right that there are three Bardos in
life and three after death, six *betweens* that bridge our
questions to our answers.

Then we cross to Yama, who will tally our dids and our
didn'ts and either seat us at the table or set us on fire.

It may be the case that the seven heavens of Behesht are
where the Zoroastrians let the soul dance while the body
rests, where the Best rise through the Star, Moon, and
Sun to Song and Endless Light.

Maybe the Wheel of Life and the Bodies of Light and
the Books of the Dead all cross the dark river and
illuminate the quiet after speaking, the sacred pause
of, *What happens now?*

It could be that the breath and the mind and the body
and the blood and the robes and the mighty hats and
the folded hands and the open hands and the bare feet
and the bowed heads are all in this together.

It may be true that reincarnation takes 45 days.
You have about six weeks to get your shit together for
a new gig, then you are gushed into existence.

You will be able to watch and wonder while around
you, hands fold blankets and mouths talk and taste
and sing, and you squint and smile through several
months of light and dark and warm baths and warm
milk and swaddling and passing of the baby, arms to
arms, like a promise that we will do better.

There is nothing truer than that we are the children
of *What Came Before* and *What Comes Next.*

No one gets to take that which connects the You to
the Us. No one has the answer to dismiss your sacred
searching.

No one holds the No that stops your lifelong Yes.

It may be true that the gates are pearly,
but those pearls are from the sea,
and the sea is always open.

The Clinic Chair Closest to the Exit
2023

the plastic has been molded
to wield both back support and seat cushion
shaped to shield your backside
from the backslide into
every last day before you're told
You're Sick

and not just any sick
the kind that makes you
count your friends
on your fingers
and your wish you hadn'ts
on your toes

14 chairs in the lobby and
you pick the burgundy one
that, maybe just maybe
might seat you farthest from
the guest that never leaves

✤ ✤ ✤

New Orleans

I come from a place
where tombs have doors

It is likely that
I have been here before

one love story

"SkelLove"
Ink on paper, 2007

Many important events happened in 2005. There were many firsts. YouTube launched on Valentine's Day. Businessman Steve Fossett became the first person to fly an airplane around the world solo without refueling, a journey of 25,000 miles completed in 67 hours and 2 minutes. Britain's Ellen MacArthur became the then-fastest person to sail a yacht solo around the world, taking 71 days, 14 hours, 18 minutes and 33 seconds. The musical Spamalot opened in New York City, ran for 1575 performances, and won three Tony Awards.

Hurricane Katrina made landfall on the Gulf Coast and caused the deaths of 1,833 people over nine days in late August. The Category 5 storm's strongest wind speed was 174 miles per hour and the costliest tropical cyclone in recorded history left over 120 billion dollars in damage, starting with the two coastal towns of Buras, Louisiana, and, in full irony, Triumph, Louisiana.

It was spring in Portland, Oregon, and we were in undergraduate classes together, each returning to school with several years of life under our belts, and enjoying a rapport filled with side-splitting laughter, assignments that grew our young minds, talking like we had 300 years of friendship between us, and the kind of listening that comes with holding something precious in your hands for the first time.

At the jump, we knew this was a friendship for the ages. We had no idea what was ahead of us. Our first class together was a capstone course about LGBTQ representation in mainstream media and movies. The first time I saw him, I thought he was a young prodigy who had found his way into a university classroom. I was impressed by how articulate and funny he was with his skateboard and backwards baseball cap. It turned out that he was only two years younger than me. There was a lot of sharing about our lives, our families, our close friends.

We were project partners for the term and wound up winning a class contest for a new marketing campaign brochure and marketing strategy for *Love Makes A Family (LMAF)*, a non-profit advocacy and assistance organization, working for equal marriage and family rights in the United States. *LMAF* was founded by the incredible Bonnie Tinker, in response to Oregon's hateful Ballot Measure 9 in 1992.

T and I worked on the project with *LMAF* in the wake of the 2004 ruling on Measure 36, which changed the Oregon constitution to specify that marriage was between one man and one woman. This discriminatory ruling stayed on the books until it was overturned in 2014.

As part of the "No on 36" project, we interviewed Katie Potter, the out and proud lesbian police officer and daughter of Mayor Tom Potter, and her then-wife Pam, at their home in Portland. They served us brunch and we played with their kids, we asked questions that they thoughtfully answered, and we organized that conversation into a pre-sentation that we were proud to deliver to our class. Bonnie Tinker came to thank us personally. It felt like the start of something important and we felt unbelievably lucky to be a part of it.

It was a year that you could go where you liked by boat or plane, as quickly as possible, to any destination that your vessel could manage. Somewhere between the 71+ days of the circumnavigating yachtswoman in February, and nature taking a one-two punch at the Gulf Coast in August, T and I began a love story.

After months of sharing what we knew—and sharing what we hoped to know about ourselves—and planning how to become healthier and more present people in the world, the gates opened and we began.

We were newly *us*, with fewer than six months to call our own. We were moving into new rentals, completing schoolwork, working full-time, with him now navigating the complexities of coparenting, and me working through *old me* stuff now that *new me* had finally arrived. It was a time of turbulence and hope. It would have been understandable to fall off the edge of those first few months, to trip over our previous decisions on the way to better ones, or faceplant in the mud of other people's expectations and opinions. No molting is tidy. We were each works in progress.

Something had changed in each of us, something powerful and sublime that reminded us daily, "You have each other now." Life kept moving forward, as it does, with incredible force and tender mercy.

My life changed the day I touched his face. It was that simple. Everything happened either before or after that moment. The protectiveness, the yearning, the gratitude, the joy, and the hope swelled in us, and despite the complicated logistics of starting out, we kept going. We showed up for each other then, and every day since.

Within the first year, I lucked out and landed an admin job at the same academic medical center where he worked, and the logistics of living well started to fall into place. I was emceeing the drag king show and involved in queer community on multiple levels as an organizer, event planner, and performer. T was parenting, working, and reconnecting with friends and family.

We were living in our individual rentals when Katrina hit New Orleans, but after work I would head to his place to get online and help the Southern family in any way that I could.

Together we aided with logistical support and tracking family members that had scattered to Arkansas, Texas, and western Louisiana. I remember looking up and seeing him working fervently on his laptop to find the name of the hotel where my mom had reserved a room but never showed, and

witnessed his investment in finding where she had gone. Twenty-four hours later she called to say that she had given the room to her sister and had landed safely elsewhere. We quietly took turns making or picking up food, talked about our days at work, went out at night with friends, and learned about each other with kind attention and adoring passion. It was a time of upheaval and incredible love.

My dad went directly north to a church community in Arkansas and found a hotel where he could hunker down and wait for the storm to pass and roads to be passable. Friends rallied and fundraised for my mom and sister, who stayed in the region in the care of a family who volunteered to help them. My previous landlord offered an apartment in southeast Portland to my brother and his then-girlfriend, and friends rallied for my brother's arrival with gift cards, clothing donations, home cooked meals, acupuncture treatments, and weekly, "What do you need? How can we help?" He stayed in the Pacific Northwest for several weeks until he got the all-clear to return.

At the height of the chaos, people had limited cell service, and no one had a stable mailing address. Medical offices were closed, and prescription medication was almost impossible to get refilled. The stress of the situation was causing myriad physical and psychological symptoms across the family. Anxiety, topical and food allergies, hypertension, tendinitis, dehydration, and sleep disruption were on heavy rotation. The news reports showed my hometown in utter chaos and devastation, and there was so little that we could do from 2,540 miles away.

My dad once said that the most important thing that happened in the family at that time was that we all had a single place for information to be collected and shared, a phone number for people to check in and ask for what they needed, a home base that chaos had not destabilized, and

that was us. We had become a force so loving and stable that the people we loved relied on us. We relied on each other without a second thought. This love was safe, nurturing, and present, with no ego or pretense.

We cared for each other's families as our own. We had date nights, special time with the kids, and solo time to take care of ourselves. We consciously tried to break patterns of behavior and toxic dynamics that had appeared in previous relationships, we owned our work and gently asked for what we needed. This love was generous and attentive, giving the benefit of the doubt and forgiving things that could happen but never did.

Everything we brought from *the before times* was left at the door. This love was a joy and a comfort, a warm blanket on a cold night and a cup of your favorite drink under a sky full of stars.

Once my family had returned to Louisiana and started the slow, grueling work of rebuilding and recentering, we settled into a life of full-time work, school, and a fifty-fifty split with half of the week parenting the incredible kids in Portland, and half the week on incredible adventures to Seattle, the Bay Area, San Diego, and Hawaii.

In these first few months, we realized that we had each been recipients of Pride Foundation scholarships prior to our relationship, him for high school athletics and me for community leadership. Years later, I wrote to the organization to share this serendipitous union of two Pride scholars, and they shared my letter with the entire staff. Within a couple of weeks, they contacted us to speak at scholarship events as a Pride Foundation success story, and asked T to give the keynote at the scholarship awards event.

We knew that there was a presence and a power to this love we had created, but we had no idea how much until it was called upon to help others and give back. We had a

love that showed up. Years passed, and a life together grew steadily beneath our feet and in front of our eyes. We rented a house in North Portland from that same magical landlord, and eventually bought an 1898 farmhouse in the same area. I was learning how to be a stepmother, how to show up fully as a partner, and how to take care of myself in a newly formed household and way of living.

We had no guidebook, but we were deeply committed to the kids and to each other. We asked for help along the way and encouraged them to ask for what they needed and to say what they thought with kindness and honesty. They grew into brilliant and beautiful young women, and we all tried to face changes with our heads up and our focus forward.

There were many challenges, and at times we were exhausted and depleted, but we were in it together. When they asked for important things or expressed complicated needs, we tried with every ounce of energy and all of our resources to find solutions. We took turns with aunts and uncles creating holiday gatherings, family calendars, and vacations. Travel was a healing and restorative force in our lives, and even now, family trips to Hawaii, the East Coast, and California remain some of our fondest memories.

Life was busy but good, with friend time and family time spent at happy hours, school events, and fixing up the house again and again, like tending a wild wooden garden that yielded the most magnificent flowers.

Three years in, and after countless ups and downs around us, we married in the summer of 2008 at Stevens Pavilion in Washington Park in Southwest Portland. The catering was from our magical landlord, who gifted us a month of no rent as a wedding present so we could have food from Nicholas Lebanese, our first date restaurant.

The good folks at Nicholas liked our first date story and were honored to be our caterer, so they gave us enough

food for double the size of our wedding party, and we donated what was left to the kitchen at Outside In, a safe, supportive, and inclusive non-profit that helps people experiencing home-lessness achieve independence.

The wine was gifted by a colleague whose family owns Yamhill Valley Vineyards, and the officiant was a dear friend from work who had helped us navigate the complexities of our new family with grace and good counsel. T's best friend was our D.J. and his best person, and my brother stood beside me, as T and I offered our full hearts to each other infront of 75 of our nearest and dearest.

My brother also busted out his disposable camera during the ceremony and took pictures of the audience while I was listening to the officiant speak of great love. You can take the guy out of New Orleans, but you can't take New Orleans out of the guy.

The family came and wished us happiness and peace. There were children dancing and toasts made. We stayed the night in a local hotel and the girls got their own room with one of their aunties whom they adore. They ordered pasta and ice cream and stayed up late. We fell asleep exhausted, but happy and laughing. The pressure was off because we had been celebrating for three years already.

The thing about queer community is that when you don't have marriage equality, which at the time we did not, you collect anniversaries in a different way.

T and I started our relationship in April, married in August, and had a small backyard ceremony in June when marriage equality became legal in Oregon. It's both gorgeous to celebrate so much, and absurd to have to multiply occasions that others only need to organize once. Queer love is a remind-er of many gifts, not the least of which are strength in numbers, resiliency, and an ability to adapt and thrive.

Years passed, and many significant life events came and went. We bought our first home, adopted a dog, moved my mom from New Orleans into our home to help her in her final years, adopted another dog, each had significant surgeries with extended healing to follow. We said final goodbyes to my first girlfriend, Traci; our dear friend, Val; T's dad, Al; T's mom, Cathy, and grandmother, Helen; my treasure of a mom, Eileen; and T's friend-mom, Anne. People came into and out of our lives and we tried to do what was needed most when it was needed most. There were many dark days from the grief and loss, but there were many celebrations of life and joyful gatherings alongside.

We tried for several years to have a child with the help of fertility specialists. Five years in and much too much money later, we shifted focus to what was next for us. Once I accepted that biological motherhood was not in the cards for me, I decided to go back to school. I got a master's in education. T got a master's in healthcare management. We kept going.

We stayed busy and kept growing together. We hosted parties and invited friends to so many things. We felt strongly that no one in our community should feel isolated or alone when our life was welcoming them, our friends were soon to be their friends, and the community that we grew together was at their fingertips. No one we know should be hungry when there is room at our table. We developed a core group of ride-or-die homies that shared the curves in the road alongside us and gave us a chance to give and take in equal measure.

T moved steadily up the management ladder at the academic medical center and I had plans to teach high school English, Social Studies, and Art, now that my newly minted teaching degree was in hand.

At my farewell party in hospital administration, a friend let me know that there would be a position opening in Child Psychiatry that seemed like a good fit, so I applied and was accepted as the first education manager for two statewide, grant-funded outreach programs. I stayed in academic medicine and became a department manager instead of a high school teacher. Years later, a position opened as the first family advocate in the organ procurement organization (OPO) servicing Oregon, Washington, and western Idaho. I applied and started what would be my new career in family advocacy and clinical education for organ donation.

Through this important work, I developed a relationship with death and dying that deepened my connections to the living, and gave my career meaning and purpose beyond anything I had known up to that point. T and I were trying new things, making enough money so that the kids were taken care of, and planning for the future.

We centered our lives around gratitude and fun as much as possible and gave back whenever we could. Once both girls graduated from high school and were in college, we decided to start fresh, since it had never been just the two of us on this adventure. Empty nesting took on a whole new meaning in a new house in a new state, 1,243 miles away from Oregon in Colorado.

Since we could work primarily remotely, we kept our jobs and planned for home offices and me traveling a portion of each month. We picked a location that had a major airport, was halfway between the kids' colleges, and had more sunshine year-round than all that Portland could muster in the 21 years that we called it home. It was one flight to everywhere that we had family, and a quick trip to work and most of our friends. We found that picking a place and planning a move was easier to do because we were easier together. We carried a home with us wherever we went, and the friends who we stayed close to after the move turned out to be the friends for the history books, or at least this history book.

So many awful things continued to happen around
the world, the horrors of the American political climate and
nationwide racism were at play alongside misogyny, religious
abuse, bigotry, and targeting of sexual and ethnic minorities.
We were a biracial, queer family in the middle of a national
hot mess that had no end in sight. We knew that we needed
to continue to be each other's strength and stay and provide
a stable landing pad for those we love, those we hoped to
help, and ourselves.

The kids grew up understanding social justice, bodily
autonomy, speaking up, asking questions, and not taking
any shit when it comes to protecting themselves or others.
They could explain things clearly and felt passionately about
topics at an early age. They had been raised by a community
of adults with hope and fury, who encouraged their develop-
ment, and provided places where they could test the waters.
They have navigated issues that are challenging for seasoned
adults. The results have been incredible to witness. They are
creative, resourceful, and self-aware. They have good friends
and strong relationships where they do their work and expect
others to do the same. We are so impressed by and proud of
them. The future is in good hands.

Today we are caring for a sick family member in our
home, and we are both working full-time. I am busy with
writing, cooking, and slowly visiting all the art and theater
in our new city. He stays busy with his woodworking side
business, hiking, and making sure that the craft beer scene
has adequate appreciation. There are still challenging days,
but none that we can't handle together. Service to those we
love, to each other, and to ourselves, moves us forward. The
best of us begets the best of us.

The most sublime part of being with the love of your
life for almost 20 years is not the looking back, or the looking

I LOVE YOU
SUPERSTAR

forward, it's the looking across the table in the home that you share. There sits love, with your best years tucked safely tucked into the crease of their clothes, every laugh and each deep sigh in their shirt pocket, and all the many questions and answers you found together stretched across their gorgeous face.

When you love someone with your entire being, there is a space created between you where every good thing is stored until it is needed: comfort, laughter, forgiveness, solutions, grace. Sometimes that space is the square footage of a house, or a farm, or an urban apartment with a rooftop garden. Sometimes that space crosses miles and it's only one call or chat or flight or sailing ship away. Sometimes you return to it at the end of the day.

Sometimes you carry the space with you, like a blanket across your shoulders, while you sip your favorite drink, under a night full of stars.

Sustenance Poetry Project** will launch with this book and create a collection of poetry submitted and work-shopped in response. We welcome any works that share the spirit of figuring it out together. Our hope is to eventually publish a collection of contributed poetry or short stories that will be used for future writing workshops.

Students and teachers can embrace the spirit of *Write Here, Write Now* with Sustenance Poetry Project, and share their work with others in group formats, in-person and online. We firmly believe that poetry should be accessible to all, and that writing is a tool in everyone's toolbox. Please send your contact information, class size, grade level, poetry previously studied by class, and three student topics of interest to the email below and we will send your class a poetry packet to be workshopped.

Email: **SustenancePoetryProject@gmail.com**
IG: **@sustenancepoetryproject**

Happy writing, friends.

We look forward to reading your work.

www.ingramcontent.com/pod-product-compliance
Lightning Source LLC
Chambersburg PA
CBHW070523160726
48003CB00004B/1680